MW00955716

Little Bible Heroes™
Solomon

Written by Victoria Kovacs
Illustrated by David Ryley

B&H KIDS
NASHVILLE, TENNESSEE

GOLDQUILL
WWW.GOLDQUILL.CO.UK

fb.com/littlebibleheroes

Published 2017 by B&H Kids, a division of LifeWay Christian Resources, Nashville, Tennessee.
Text and illustrations copyright © 2017, GoldQuill, United Kingdom.
All rights reserved. Scripture quotations are taken from the Christian Standard Bible ®
Copyright © 2017 by Holman Bible Publishers. Used by permission.
ISBN: 978-1-4627-4337-7   Dewey Decimal Classification: CE
Subject Heading: SOLOMON, KING OF ISRAEL \ JONAH \ BIBLE STORIES
Printed in May 2017 in Shenzhen, Guangdong, China
21 20 19 18 17 • 1 2 3 4 5

King David has a son. His name is Solomon. He is crowned the king of Israel.

God is happy with Solomon's answer. God says, "I will give you wisdom as you asked. I will also give you what you didn't ask for—riches and honor. While you live, no king will be greater than you."

Solomon builds God's temple. It is a magnificent building. The walls, floor, and doors inside the temple are covered in pure gold.

The queen of Sheba hears about Solomon. She travels from far, far away to see the king. She brings him gold, spices, and jewels.

The queen is amazed
by how rich and wise
King Solomon is.

People from all over the world want to meet King Solomon and hear the wisdom God has given him.

Read:

So God said to him, . . . "I will give you a wise and understanding heart, so that there has never been anyone like you before and never will be again. In addition, I will give you what you did not ask for: both riches and honor."—1 Kings 3:11–13

Think:

1. Solomon asked God for wisdom. What have you asked God for?
2. Why is wisdom a good gift?

Remember:

Ask God for what you need. He is listening!

Read:

I called to the L<small>ORD</small> in my distress, and he answered me. I cried out for help. . . . you heard my voice.—Jonah 2:2

Think:

1. When have you asked God for help?
2. The people of Nineveh changed and did the right thing. Are you happy when people do the right thing?

Remember:

When we ask God for help, He hears us.

In the morning, the plant dies.
Jonah grows very hot and complains.

God asks him, "Why are you angry?
You care about the plant. Shouldn't I
care about the people of Nineveh?"

All the people are sorry and turn to God. Even the king! But Jonah is angry. He sits down outside the city to see what will happen to it.

God causes a plant to grow to shade Jonah's head while he waits.

Now Jonah goes to Nineveh. He tells the people God will destroy the city if the people do not repent.

Jonah prays to God for help.
The fish spits Jonah out on land.

God sends a big fish to swallow Jonah!

For three days and three nights,
Jonah is in the fish's belly.

God sends a big storm. The
sailors are scared. Jonah
tells them to throw him
overboard to calm the sea.

Jonah doesn't obey God. Instead, he gets on a ship going the other way.

Jonah is a prophet. God tells him, "Go to the city of Nineveh. Warn the people that I have seen their wickedness."

Little Bible Heroes™
Jonah

Written by Victoria Kovacs
Illustrated by David Ryley

B&H KIDS
NASHVILLE, TENNESSEE

GOLDQUILL
WWW.GOLDQUILL.CO.UK

fb.com/littlebibleheroes

Published 2017 by B&H Kids, a division of LifeWay Christian Resources, Nashville, Tennessee.
Text and illustrations copyright © 2017, GoldQuill, United Kingdom.
All rights reserved. Scripture quotations are taken from the Christian Standard Bible ®
Copyright © 2017 by Holman Bible Publishers. Used by permission.
ISBN: 978-1-4627-4337-7   Dewey Decimal Classification: CE
Subject Heading: SOLOMON, KING OF ISRAEL \ JONAH \ BIBLE STORIES
Printed in May 2017 in Shenzhen, Guangdong, China
21 20 19 18 17 • 1 2 3 4 5